30-Day Empowerment Journal
A GUIDE TO DARE! LIVE! & BE!
By: Te'Ara Arman

This Journal Belongs to:

_____

Copyright © 2021 Te'Ara Arman

All rights reserved.

WWW.TEARAARMAN.COM
ISBN:978-0-578-87545-3

Introduction

Through life we have many negatives stacked against us which is what makes us stronger and guides us to success. That Success begins when we "Dare to be different". As we are being different, we are stepping out of the cookie cutter path and taking chances to create our own. Of course, this means we may stand alone at times as we develop and grow into successful people who "Live to Inspire" others to believe and invest in themselves to do the same. With the investment, vulnerability is shown, and you get to "Be exactly who you are".

- Te'Ara Arman

Inspiration

In the next 30 days you will break down what dare to be different, live to inspire and be who you are means to you. During this time, you will explore some growth in yourself that you did not know existed. It will be extremely exciting, challenging, new, overwhelming at times and overcoming. Some days will be tougher than others. Your confidence and self-worth will be tested, and it is especially important that you accept and recite W.I.S.D.O.M. Welcome Innovative Soulful & Distinguished One Hundred Percent Meritorious daily!

Date_____

Day One

Before you can jump into figuring out what Dare! Live! Be! means to you, you must realize what holds you back. To do that, ask yourself what is your biggest fear?

_____
_____
_____
_____
_____
_____
_____
_____
_____
_____
_____
_____

Date_____

Day Two

We all have fears that keep us from reaching our highest potential. What happened in your life that made you feel that you were not worthy to reach your potential in life or business?

_____
_____
_____
_____
_____
_____
_____
_____
_____
_____
_____
_____
_____
_____
_____
_____

Date_____

Day Three

Dare to be different means to step out on faith and take a chance. Step out of that cookie cutter path and create your own lane. Take a few minutes and think about the word dare. What does dare mean to you?

_____
_____
_____
_____
_____
_____
_____
_____
_____
_____
_____
_____

Date_____

Day Four

When you hear dare to be different, what are some things that come to mind?

_____
_____
_____
_____
_____
_____
_____
_____
_____
_____
_____
_____
_____
_____
_____
_____
_____

Date_____

Day Five

What are some challenges you have when you dare to be different?

_____
_____
_____
_____
_____
_____
_____
_____
_____
_____
_____
_____
_____
_____
_____
_____
_____

Date_____

Day Six

How have you dared to be different today? What were some challenges? How did you overcome them?

_____
_____
_____
_____
_____
_____
_____
_____
_____
_____
_____
_____
_____
_____
_____
_____
_____

Date_____

Day Seven

How have you dared to be different today? What were some challenges? How did you overcome them?

_____
_____
_____
_____
_____
_____
_____
_____
_____
_____
_____
_____
_____
_____
_____
_____

Date_____

Day Eight

How have you dared to be different today? What were some challenges? How did you overcome them?

_____

_____

_____

_____

_____

_____

_____

_____

_____

_____

_____

_____

_____

_____

_____

Date_____

Day Nine

How have you dared to be different today? What were some challenges? How did you overcome them?

Date_____

Day Ten

How have you dared to be different today? What were some challenges? How did you overcome them?

_____
_____
_____
_____
_____
_____
_____
_____
_____
_____
_____
_____
_____
_____
_____

Date_____

Day 11

Congratulations let's reflect.

You have completed the first 10 days on your journey to Dare! Live! Be! Take a little time to reflect and write about your successes below.

_____
_____
_____
_____
_____
_____
_____
_____
_____
_____
_____
_____
_____
_____

Date_____

Day 12-Inspiration

It's okay to make a mistake as long as you learn from it.

Notes

Date_____

Day Thirteen

Live to Inspire means to give someone the courage and tools they need to be successful. Remember it is okay to bring someone on the success train with you to empower them to follow their dreams. What does inspire mean to you?

_____
_____
_____
_____
_____
_____
_____
_____
_____
_____
_____
_____

Date_____

Day Fourteen

When you hear live to inspire, what are some things that come to mind?

_____
_____
_____
_____
_____
_____
_____
_____
_____
_____
_____
_____
_____
_____
_____
_____
_____

Date_____

Day Fifteen

What are some challenges with living to inspire?

Date_____

Day Sixteen

How have you lived to inspire today? What were some challenges? How did you overcome them?

_____
_____
_____
_____
_____
_____
_____
_____
_____
_____
_____
_____
_____
_____
_____
_____

Date_____

Day Seventeen

How have you lived to inspire today? What were some challenges? How did you overcome them?

_____
_____
_____
_____
_____
_____
_____
_____
_____
_____
_____
_____
_____
_____
_____
_____
_____

Date_____

Day Eighteen

How have you lived to inspire today? What were some challenges? How did you overcome them?

_____
_____
_____
_____
_____
_____
_____
_____
_____
_____
_____
_____
_____
_____
_____

Date_____

Day Nineteen

How have you lived to inspire today? What were some challenges? How did you overcome them?

Date_____

Day Twenty

How have you lived to inspire today? What were some challenges? How did you overcome them?

_____
_____
_____
_____
_____
_____
_____
_____
_____
_____
_____
_____
_____

Date_____

Day Twenty-One

Congratulations let's reflect.

You have completed the 20 days on your journey to Dare! Live! Be! Take a little time to reflect and write about your successes below.

_____
_____
_____
_____
_____
_____
_____
_____
_____
_____
_____
_____
_____
_____

Date_____

Day Twenty-Two
T.R.U.S.T.

TOTALLY
RELY
UPON YOUR
SELF
TRUTH

Notes

Date_____

Day Twenty-Three

Being who you are means to be authentically who you are meant to be and live in your purpose. Be sure to accept everything about you flaws and all. Those are the things that make you so great. Think about it, when you hear be who you are, what comes to mind?

_____
_____
_____
_____
_____
_____
_____
_____
_____
_____
_____
_____
_____

Date_____

Day Twenty-Four

What are some of your strengths and how can they help you grow?

_____
_____
_____
_____
_____
_____
_____
_____
_____
_____
_____
_____
_____
_____
_____
_____

Date_____

Day Twenty-Five

What are some of your weaknesses and how can they help you grow?

_____
_____
_____
_____
_____
_____
_____
_____
_____
_____
_____
_____
_____
_____
_____
_____
_____

Date_____

Day Twenty-Six

How have you been authentically "you" today? What were some challenges? How did you overcome them?

_____
_____
_____
_____
_____
_____
_____
_____
_____
_____
_____
_____
_____
_____
_____

Date_____

Day Twenty-Seven

How have you been authentically "you" today? What were some challenges? How did you overcome them?

_____
_____
_____
_____
_____
_____
_____
_____
_____
_____
_____
_____
_____
_____
_____
_____
_____
_____

Date_____

Day Twenty-Eight

How have you been authentically "you" today? What were some challenges? How did you overcome them?

_____
_____
_____
_____
_____
_____
_____
_____
_____
_____
_____
_____
_____
_____
_____
_____

Date_____

Day Twenty-Nine

How have you been authentically "you" today? What were some challenges? How did you overcome them?

_____
_____
_____
_____
_____
_____
_____
_____
_____
_____
_____
_____
_____
_____

Date_____

Day Thirty

How have you been authentically "you" today? What were some challenges? How did you overcome them?

_____
_____
_____
_____
_____
_____
_____
_____
_____
_____
_____
_____
_____
_____

Date_____

Congratulations let's reflect.

You have completed the final 10 days on your journey to Dare! Live! Be! Take a little time to reflect and write about the lessons you learned and your successes below.

_____
_____
_____
_____
_____
_____
_____
_____
_____
_____
_____
_____
_____
_____

Date_____

CONGRATULATIONS

You made it through!
Dare! Live! & Be!
Say it with me!
I will Dare to be different!
I will live to Inspire!
I will be exactly who I am!

Date_____

COMMITTMENT

I, _____ am committed to dare, live and be every day.

Signed,

_____

Reflections

REMEMBER

SELF EMPOWERMENT LEADS TO FREEDOM INDEPENDENCE EXCELLENCE

ABOUT THE AUTHOR

Hey everyone! I am Author, International Speaker, Purpose Coach and Podcast Host, Te'Ara Arman who is passionate about helping, supporting, mentoring, and guiding others to their potential. Committed to proactively create innovative methods of empowerment so that we may continue to approach our lives with self confidence as we dare to be different, live to inspire and be who we are.

Thank you so much for going on this Dare! Live! Be! journey with me.

Follow us on IG/FB/TW @tearaspeaks to be in the know of what is to come. To inquire about booking email info@tearaarman.com.

www.tearaarman.com

Made in the USA
Columbia, SC
09 August 2023